A SECOND BOOK OF
EXCITING
SENTENCES

BY ALAN PEAT & MATHEW SULLIVAN

CREATIVE EDUCATIONAL PRESS LTD

PUBLISHED BY: Creative Educational Press Ltd
2 The Walled Garden
Grange Park Drive
Biddulph
Staffs
ST8 7TA

Tel: 07789938923
Fax: 01782 379398

PRINTED BY: York Publishing Services Ltd.,
64, Hallfield Road, Layerthorpe, York, YO31 7ZQ

DESIGN: Simon Matthews

PROOFREADING: Angela Burt and Tom Storey

Alan Peat   www.alanpeat.com
info@alanpeat.com

Mathew Sullivan   mathew@inspiredminds.eu

Simon Matthews   www.s2air.co.uk
info@s2air.co.uk

ISBN: 9780957079663

Also available from Creative Educational Press Ltd (www.thecepress.com):

Writing Exciting Sentences: Age 7 Plus by Alan Peat
50 Ways to Retell a Story: Cinderella by Alan Peat, Julie Peat and Christopher Storey
Get Your Head Around Punctuation (...and how to teach it!) by Alan Peat
The Elves and The Shoemaker 1897 illustrated by John Harrold
Writing Exciting Ghost Stories: Age 9 Plus: Ghost Story Plot Skeletons by Alan Peat
(co-author Julie Barnfather)
Teaching Outstanding Persuasive Writing by Alan Peat
Developing Writing Through Comics by Mathew Sullivan
The Magic Stone by Alan Peat (illustrated by John Harrold)
Word Warriors (CD-ROM Game) design by Simon Matthews
Spelling Bee (CD-ROM Game) design by Simon Matthews

ALAN PEAT @alanpeat

Alan Peat is a Staffordshire based Independent Education Consultant with a national and international reputation for training which has an immediate, sustainable impact on literacy standards. Teachers from across the UK comment on how much children ENJOY writing as a result of Alan's techniques and approaches being used in the classroom.

His achievements have led to the award of a Fellowship of the Royal Society of Arts (F.R.S.A.) in 2003 and, most recently, a Fellowship of the Historical Association (F.H.A.) '...in recognition of a significant contribution to the promotion and knowledge of history.' (October 2010)

Alan's work is now being used in 22 countries.

Thanks:

To my wife Julie for all her editorial support and many contributing ideas. I'd be lost without her!

Thanks also to my Mum and Dad for their unwavering support and love, and to Simon Matthews for his superb design work and friendship. Angela Burt and Tom Storey also deserve praise for their excellent proofreading.

Finally, many thanks to Mathew for his outstanding contributions, and his friendship.

MATHEW SULLIVAN @InspiredMind5

Mathew Sullivan is a class teacher and Literacy Co-ordinator at St. Richard's R.C. Primary School, Manchester. He provides CPD training for Manchester Metropolitan University on using comics to enhance literacy teaching. This has been evaluated as 'superb' and 'inspiring' by attendees. Mathew also works as a creative and pedagogic consultant for the University's Comic SMART initiative and his techniques are implemented in secondary schools across Manchester.

Mathew has showcased his techniques and approaches in schools across the North West. His book, *Developing Writing Through Comics* will be published by Creative Educational Press Ltd later this year. He was graded 'outstanding' by Ofsted in 2013 and named Silk 106.9 Teacher of the Year in 2012.

Thanks:

To the staff and pupils of St. Richard's for their inspiration.

Thanks to my family and friends for their support.

Thanks to Alan for the opportunity.

Thanks to my Nan for the best example of determination, hard work and spirit anyone could ever ask for.

INTRODUCTION _____ P.2

SENTENCES

INTRODUCTION

The children in my class love them. Children who were disengaged with the technicalities of writing are now enthused and confident...
(Andrew Robinson, Shiphay Learning Academy)

When the children are spotting these sentences in other writing, then you know they've cracked it. A brilliant book that helps children improve their writing by providing a framework for their sentences. My children LOVE it.
(@MrPlaceICT)

Your sentences are outstanding, outstanding because they encourage children to be creative and play with language.
(@RobW1976)

Your sentences approach left my 'difficult' boys begging to write. A clear success! I'd recommend to all.
(@jogyouon)

The sentences book revolutionised the way we taught grammar in my school and the increase in the quality of writing is immense.
(@redgierob)

Your sentences helped move our children from 0% Level 5 to 50% Level 5 writers but, more importantly, it moved them from disengaged, unmotivated and unenthused to motivated, engaged and successful.
(@Janey23HT)

Mr Peat, thank you so much for creating such exciting sentences.
(Ellie Wright, Mrs Gold's class, Dial Park Primary School, Stockport)

ALAN'S INTRODUCTION

In my first publication on this subject (*Writing Exciting Sentences: Age 7 Plus*, Creative Educational Press Ltd 2008) I explained that my intention was to '...help pupils to write more varied sentences which engage and captivate the reader'. The book is now our most popular publication, and ideas contained within it are being used effectively in over 20 countries. I receive emails and tweets about the sentences book on a daily basis. Some typical examples are included opposite.

After such an overwhelmingly positive response, I thought long and hard about producing a second book of sentence types. I did not want to produce another book until I had gathered sufficient new sentence types which were of equal quality to those in the first volume. However, after discussing the project with Mathew Sullivan it was clear that he also had a passion for the approach, and after he completed his book *Developing Writing Through Comics*, we agreed to co-author this text. I am now confident that between us we have written a second book of (at least) equal worth! We've even included 'guest pages' at the back of this book, with new sentence types suggested by both teachers and pupils. Many thanks to all those who took the trouble to write to me. We have included as many as possible!

However, as more than five years have elapsed since the launch of the first book, there are several key points I wish to raise regarding HOW the sentence types should, and should not, be taught.

Firstly, they should NOT be taught in a decontextualised manner: a whole lesson practising a sentence type which has been divorced from context would be a pedagogically regressive move. Rather, they should be explored and explicitly discussed using shared and guided reading as an introductory vehicle e.g. finding a sentence type within a text currently being read, followed by explicit reference to the sentence type's simple name (e.g. 2A sentence). After naming the sentence type there should be an explanation of the name (e.g. 2A stands for 2 adjectives before the noun) and then, most importantly, a discussion about WHY the writer has used the sentence type at that particular point within the text (e.g. to create a clear 'visual impression' of a character for the reader).

This exploration of **when** and **why** sentence types are used is of fundamental importance and needs whole-school discussion during both staff meetings and INSET days. Some sentence types are inappropriate for certain genres. Take, for example, 'Personification of Weather', from the first book. Although this sentence type is incredibly useful when aiming to create a specific mood in the context of narrative writing (*The rain wept down the window* - sad mood) it is wholly inappropriate in the context of an instructional text. This issue of 'fitness for purpose' should be explored by ALL staff in schools using the sentence types.

After introducing sentence types through discussion of their usage in shared and guided reading, the next step is to encourage pupils to apply/use the sentence types as SUBTARGETS in engaging writing sessions:

KEY TARGET: To write a scary ghost story
SUBTARGET: To use 2A sentences when first introducing a new character or place so that the reader can 'see' them more easily.

I have audited, trained and taught in many hundreds of schools since 2008 and it has become clear that, in schools where the sentence types are having the most readily quantifiable positive impact, six key factors are usually firmly in place. I have outlined these opposite for ease of use.

THE SIX KEYS TO SUCCESSFUL WHOLE SCHOOL APPLICATION OF SENTENCE TYPES

1 All staff agree and use the same terminology to describe sentence types (e.g. If the Year 2 teacher talks about a 2A sentence then the Year 3 teacher should also call it a 2A sentence etc).

This whole-school 'consistent language' approach is of paramount importance.

Note that if the school has a transient population of staff, then the Senior Management Team need to have systems in place which ensure that new staff (NQT's etc) are mentored with regard to the school's agreed 'consistent language' policy. If this does not occur, time will rapidly dilute impact.

2 All staff use reading sessions as vehicles for the discussion of sentence types (...though NOT every time pupils read or are read to - they should also be encouraged to read purely for pleasure).

3 Sentence types are matched to text types - all staff should be involved in this process as it upskills teachers, as well as promoting active discussion of the subject.

4 Sentence types are then applied as subtargets (as discussed previously) in engaging writing sessions. These sessions should, as often as possible, have both real purposes and real audiences.

5 All staff recognise and accept that initially (though not in the long term!) the 'flow' of pupils' writing may be interrupted when they first begin to apply sentence types. This is a temporary, developmental stage which also occurs when overt punctuation targets are set.

6 The application of sentence types is NOT turned into an overly prescriptive 'numbers game'. (Some pupils will, however, challenge themselves in this manner - setting themselves targets. The importance of text flow should be discussed with these pupils, but they should also be allowed to play/experiment with the sentence types.) Pupils should never be told to apply a fixed number of sentence types when writing. In successful schools there has been a far greater emphasis on **when** and **why** sentence types are used. These two w's are of central importance.

In this volume I have been fortunate to work with Mathew Sullivan, a friend/teacher whom I hold in high regard. Between us we have found thirty 'new' sentence types (the sentence types in both books have all been derived from texts we have read!) and given each a simple name for both staff and pupils to use consistently.

Our aim when using 'simple language' to name sentence types is NOT to be simplistic, but rather to engage younger pupils (for whom the complex metalanguage of sentences may be either inappropriate or off-putting) in the process of discussing and thinking about a broad range of sentence types. This is a direct precursor to children applying a broad range of sentence types in their own writing. Later discussion of appropriate metalanguage is NOT precluded and is more likely to be retained if the pupil is an enthusiastic writer of sentences.

We do NOT expect - or want - pupils to rote-learn the combined fifty-five sentence types in the two books. When writing this second volume we merely sought to widen the range from which pupils and teachers might choose...regardless of the genre being explored.

This book is entirely co-written and co-edited with Mathew Sullivan and I trust that readers will find that this two-pronged approach has helped to create a second volume which is both rooted in outstanding classroom practice and also readily transferable to a broad range of school contexts.

Alan Peat. August 2013

MATHEW'S INTRODUCTION

Like a significant number of other teachers, I first encountered the *Exciting Sentences* on a training day run by Alan Peat. As a result of that one-day experience, it was clear how effective the approach could be, and how this unique system had the potential to develop the writing ability of all pupils.

Sure enough, the next day I was introducing the first of Alan's sentence types, and found my expectations were entirely justified. Not only did pupils find the naming system and subsequent word patterning helpful (facilitating quick independent usage), but they also 'got' the idea of the system as a whole.

Needless to say, the striking difference in the pupils' writing soon caught the attention of other teachers, and the SLT. So much so that a significant part of my Literacy Coordinator role was taken up with implementing *Exciting Sentences* as part of a whole-school approach to writing. The idea was that, year-upon-year, pupils would learn new *Exciting Sentences* in the context of their topic/modular work. By Year 6, they would have the full arsenal of sentence types at their disposal. This is exactly how things progressed and, within the first year of this whole-school approach, some pupils achieved Level 6 in their writing and percentage results for Level 4 and 5 were way above the national average - a great result for any school, and an outstanding result for an inner-city school like ours. Thanks to the inclusion of the sentence types in our whole-school approach, writing results have remained consistently high ever since.

Although assessed results are important, personally I was most happy to see the effect the sentences had on the confidence and engagement of pupils at every ability level, regardless of gender. High-ability pupils relished the *Exciting Sentences*: manipulating them, combining them, breaking the established rules and even creating their own patterns. Middle-ability pupils finally felt like they had a clear way to make their writing more polished and varied. They felt more able to experiment with both vocabulary and punctuation due to their newfound confidence. Lower-ability pupils found writing much less intimidating, knowing that if they became 'stuck' then they could call upon an *Exciting Sentence* to give form and structure to the ideas they so desperately wanted to get down on paper.

The sentences even helped to increase reading and comprehension skills, as each day pupils would enthusiastically show me the sentences they had found in their reading books. Not only did this boost their confidence (as they saw themselves using the same literacy constructions as respected authors), but it enabled them to become more analytical and involved in their reading. Pupils would often ask, "Is this an exciting sentence?" and what they had actually done was spot a grammatical technique used in one of the sentence types (e.g. a subordinate clause, as used in a noun, who/which/where sentence). This enabled group discussions regarding the technical aspects of the sentences, including the use of metalanguage where appropriate. The resultant learning from these discussions could then be applied in writing sessions.

After experiencing these successes in applying the *Exciting Sentences* approach, I was thrilled to be asked to contribute to a new book by my friend and mentor, Alan Peat. Having just completed a book on using comics to develop literacy skills with his publishing company (Creative Educational Press Ltd), I jumped at the opportunity to join him on this subsequent venture.

As Alan has mentioned, the thinking behind this book, first and foremost, was to produce a new selection of *Exciting Sentences* of equal, if not greater quality, to expand both teacher and pupil choice. We also wanted to help teachers as much as possible by enabling them to use the sentences as a vehicle for teaching a range of punctuation and grammatical techniques. (Another success of the whole-school *Exiting Sentences* approach as applied in my school was that, even before the SPAG tests were introduced, spelling, punctuation and grammar techniques and terms were already being taught, in context, and pupils were confident in their usage. Of the first group of pupils to take the test, 79% achieved Level 5 and above, with a significant number achieving Level 6. Whatever your views on the SPAG tests, we see these learning opportunities as incredibly useful!)

We also believed it important to include some non-standard forms, so that pupils could explore and have fun with them. The pedants may not approve, but enabling pupils to develop their own unique stylistic approach, whilst ensuring structural coherence and written accuracy, is an integral part of higher-level writing.

Throughout this book we have focused on usability and versatility - creating new *Exciting Sentences* which are simple to grasp, manipulate, combine and apply in a wide variety of contexts. To this end, we have included a range of examples for each sentence type, adding links to different genres and text types, as well as simplified examples which might prove useful when first introducing the sentences. We have also included a trial text, comprised solely of *Exciting Sentences*, to aid teachers in their efforts to teach the sentences in **context**. As Alan has often pointed out, and as I myself advocate, these sentences must be taught in context. Using them as subtargets within independent writing activities is a crucial factor in making them as effective and useful as possible.

Above all, we have tried to make these new *Exciting Sentences* EXCITING! It may sound obvious, but we believe the real key to the success of this approach is pupil motivation. They engage readers and inspire pupils - writers improve and progress because they are excited by the prospect of learning and correctly applying the sentences they know, and writing becomes what it should be...fun!

Mathew Sullivan. August 2013

1 TELL: SHOW 3; EXAMPLES SENTENCES

EXAMPLES

He was feeling relaxed: shoes off; shirt undone; lying on the sofa.

James was happy: flashing a smile; skipping along; waving his hands.

The commander was tense: sweat dripping; eyes narrowed; staring out on to the battlefield.
(Narrative. Character description)

It was a sleepy town: shops shuttered; cats lazing in the shade; dogs snoozing in the sun.
(Narrative. Location description)

EXPLANATION

This is a two-part sentence. The first part **tells** the reader a broad-ranging fact/opinion about a subject.

He was feeling relaxed

This is followed by a colon which demonstrates that a list of **examples** will follow.

He was feeling relaxed:

After the colon the list of **3 examples** follows (in this instance actions which show that the person is relaxed).

He was feeling relaxed: shoes off; shirt undone; lying on the sofa.

As this is a phrase list (rather than single words) semicolons are used between the details rather than commas.

TEACHING TIPS AND GENRE LINKS

In terms of character description, this sentence builds on the idea of 'show-not-tell' (describing a character or mood through action - showing!). Once the initial descriptive phrase is established, drama provides an ideal vehicle for drawing out the manifestations of the characteristic. For example, if the initial phrase is Jack was terrified – pupils might explore that emotion physically in order to identify the listed examples.

Jack was terrified: **pulse racing; palms sweating; shaking uncontrollably.**

This technique encourages pupils to think about ways in which they might convey characteristics succinctly through carefully selected vocabulary presented in the correct tense.

When teaching this sentence type we find it best to provide pupils with a short list of two or three 'Tell statements' (the first part of this sentence type) such as,

She was in a bad mood:

It was a busy city:

The sea is full of life:

Pupils then 'brainstorm' examples (actions which show they are in a bad mood; facets of a busy city etc.) and the teacher, acting as a scribe, models how to turn these into **Tell: show 3; examples** sentences. The pupils are then asked to include an example as a subtarget within the genre they are writing.

EXTENSION

More confident writers might develop the sophistication of this sentence by increasing the complexity/subtlety of the initial description and thus the language of the **examples** e.g.

The audience was captivated: fingers gripped armrests tightly; eyes were wide as saucers; hearts raced, waiting to see what would happen.

(Note the use of a simile in the examples list.)

FURTHER EXAMPLES

Henry VIII was a ruthless king: divorcing unwanted wives; beheading others; executing many who opposed him.

Felix Baumgartner was ready: equipment detached; safety checks complete; waiting to drop back to Earth.
(History: Report or possibly persuasive genre)

Van Gogh painted a variety of subjects: blazing flowers; vivid landscapes; atmospheric portraits etc.
(Art: Biographical recount)

The rainforest has a huge range of flora and fauna: creeping vines; howling monkeys; birds with long, bright tail feathers etc.
(Geography: Report)

14

2 BROKEN SENTENCES

EXAMPLES

You horrible. Little. Man!

Complete. And utter. Fool!
(Narrative or Playscript - Negative)

Enormous. Juicy. Hamburger!

No. Flipping. Way!
(Narrative or Playscript - Positive)

EXPLANATION

Broken sentences mimic the way people speak and are used to indicate a strong emotion on behalf of the speaker, such as astonishment, surprise, anger or happiness. The strong emotion can be either positive or negative, as the four examples indicate.

Broken sentences are essentially three-part sentences which usually begin with two related adjectives, both of which describe the subject of the sentence (the subject being the last word of the sentence).

You horrible little man!

However, if this is turned into a broken sentence then full stops are placed after each of the separate elements.

You horrible. Little. Man!

The breaking up of the sentence adds dramatic emphasis to each element.

TEACHING TIPS AND GENRE LINKS

When teaching this sentence type, we suggest that the broken sentence is spoken out loud with a sufficient dramatic pause between each element. This will help pupils to hear how the sentence sounds, an important factor in its correct usage.

This sentence type is most useful in narrative as an aspect of direct speech. It is also useful when writing comics and it can be used in playscripts by either the characters or the narrator (as a form of authorial intrusion).

We also advise that the sentence type is not overused or its impact is quickly negated. It is advisable to explain to pupils that broken sentences are often separated from the surrounding text, as paragraphs themselves.

EXTENSION

Once established via dialogue, this sentence type may be taken out of the 'familiar' context of speech and used to form a repetition sentence (not unlike a 'First word last' sentence - see page 34) to emphasise the gravity of a situation as perceived by either a character or the omniscient narrator.

They decided to venture on. It was a mistake. A terrible. Dreaded. Mistake.

A variant is to use the same process to emphasise the positive nature of a situation as perceived by a character or the omniscient narrator.

The princess was delighted. Absolutely. Positively. Delighted!

FURTHER EXAMPLES

Tough. Horrible. Day!
(Diary)

Stop. Right. There!
(Narrative: command - a useful variant)

Fantastic. Sunny. Morning!
(Narrative: dialogue)

3

ITALICS 'STRESSED WORD' SENTENCES

EXAMPLES

1. John walked to the second floor window and leaned out as far as he could to watch the birds in the garden below. His mother looked at him in horror.
"John, *please.*"
(The italicised/stressed word indicates a strong emotion - in this instance 'concern'.)

2. John reached over the table and took a handful of chocolate cake. He shoved it into his mouth with his sticky fingers.
"John, *please.*"
OR
"John, *don't.*"
OR
"John, *no!*"
(The italicised/stressed word indicates a strong emotion - in this instance 'disgust'/ 'anger'.)

3. John told his mum that he thought Newcastle United would win both the Premiership and the F.A. Cup.
"John, *please.*"
(The italicised/stressed word indicates a strong emotion - in this instance 'disbelief'.)

EXPLANATION

This sentence type occurs in written dialogue and (like the previous sentence type) helps the reader to 'hear' how a word is being spoken. The use of italics is a stylistic convention which indicates that the speaker is emphasising the word. In this sense the italics help to indicate the cadences of speech.

In the examples (opposite and overleaf) the actual sentence type can be found at the end of the passage (first three) or the start of the passage (last three). In all six examples the extended passage demonstrates the crucial importance of context.

TEACHING TIPS AND GENRE LINKS

This sentence type is useful for introducing stylistic, graphological conventions. It is most easily taught through speaking and listening exercises. You might, for example, display sentences that have not yet been italicised, then provide pupils with a dramatic context and let THEM identify the stressed word by recognising it in their own intonation. There are also grammatical teaching links to be made with sentence types which use imperatives, use of ICT formatting skills, and reading with expression.

It is perhaps wise to discuss with pupils how this sentence type does not adhere to rigid definitions of 'correct grammar'. It is, however, used successfully by many established modern novelists and we have therefore chosen to include it.

This sentence type is applicable within the context of both narrative genres and playscripts. It also occurs in comic book dialogue.

EXTENSION

Expand the use of stylistic features for emphasis by exploring the use of bold type for key words.

When water vapour cools to form clouds, it is called **condensation**.

The sign displayed just one single word: **Danger**.

FURTHER EXAMPLES

4. *"Please* don't!" screamed Jessica.
(The italicised/stressed word indicates a strong emotion - in this instance 'desperation'.)

5. "You *must* not venture into the ruins," protested the wise old shaman.
(The italicised/stressed word indicates a strong emotion - in this instance 'fear'.)

6. Churchill *had* to come up with a new strategy, otherwise the campaign would be lost.
(In this variant, having been removed from the context of dialogue, the italicised/stressed word demonstrates how imperative the action is.)

4 OBJECT/PERSON (aka...) SENTENCES

EXAMPLES

The brave policeman (aka P.C. No-nonsense) rounded up the mean bullies.

John Wilson (aka The Bonecrusher) seemed quite ordinary when you first met him.
(Narrative)

Jesse James (aka Tom Howard) was one of the most feared outlaws of the Wild West.
(Report/Biographical recount)

EXPLANATION

In this sentence type aka (ay-kay-ay) is an abbreviation meaning "also known as".

It was originally used by lawyers and journalists to specify an alias, but now has a much wider usage as the examples demonstrate.

It can also be used figuratively and sarcastically.

My dad (aka the worst cook in England) entered the kitchen with a smile on his face.

TEACHING TIPS AND GENRE LINKS

This sentence may be introduced by inventing or locating alternative names (such as nicknames) or simply by adding alternative terms.

Police officers (aka bobbies) have a very tough job to do.

The 'aka' section of the sentence is an embedded/subordinate clause and, as such, can be separated from the rest of the sentence with **EITHER** brackets OR commas.

My dad, aka the worst cook in England, entered the kitchen with a smile on his face.

Neither is incorrect: it is merely a style preference.

EXTENSION

The sentence type can be used as a vehicle for providing additional information regarding the alternative names for inanimate objects or topics.

A good grill pan (aka griddle or chargrill) is an essential item of kitchen equipment.

(Instruction or Explanation)

Russia (aka the Russian Federation) once had a great and far-reaching empire.

(Historical or Geographical report)

FURTHER EXAMPLES

The alien species (aka the Blorgons) invaded Earth in the year 2156.
(Narrative: Science Fiction genre)

Number 27 (aka The Old Wilson House) was a place feared by every child of that neighbourhood.
(Narrative: Ghost story)

Robert Smith (aka Light-fingered Bob) was a notorious pickpocket.
(Narrative: Detective story)

5

NAME - ADJECTIVE PAIR - SENTENCES

EXAMPLES

Little Tim - happy and generous - was always fun to be around.

Ben Roberts - weak and nervy - was actually a secret superhero.
(Narrative)

Achilles - fiery and ferocious - led the Myrmidons through the formidable Trojan defences.
(Historical report)

EXPLANATION

This sentence works on a show AND tell basis, where the **name** and **details** form the main clause –

Achilles led the Myrmidons through the formidable Trojan defences. (show)

- and are separated and explained by the qualities described in the **adjective pair.**

Achilles - fiery and ferocious - led the Myrmidons through the formidable Trojan defences. (show and tell)

TEACHING TIPS AND GENRE LINKS

Pupils often find it easy to suggest character traits (which may be used to form a word bank for the adjective pair) but the rest of the sentence allows them to explore actions which result from these traits. This sentence can also be used as a basis for teaching that clauses can also be separated using dashes rather than commas or brackets, thus expanding the range of punctuation used.

EXTENSION

Challenge pupils to apply the sentence pattern to objects, animals and concepts to broaden its usage:

Glass - fragile and dangerous - must be handled with care.

(Explanation)

Recycling - household and industrial - is a crucial element in conserving our environment.

(Report or Persuasive)

Rats - unsanitary and flea-ridden - were thought to have carried the Bubonic Plague.

(Historical report)

If adjectives are changed to verbs, another variant is achieved:

David - screaming and shouting - ran from the house with his underpants on his head.

(Narrative)

The trees - swaying and swishing - made the summer evening seem ever so peaceful.

(Narrative)

SAME WORD END OF 2 SENTENCES

6

EXAMPLES

*My brother and I did everything **together**. We went to school, ate, swam, laughed and cried **together**.*

*The work was **hard**. It was depressingly, horribly, unbelievably **hard**.*
(Narrative)

*Polluting our oceans is both a long and a short term **mistake**. For both the flora and fauna of our oceans it is already a calamitous **mistake**.*
(Persuasive writing)

EXPLANATION

This sentence type is similar to the yoked sentence from the first book of sentence types. In a yoked sentence the last word of one sentence becomes the first word of the next sentence.

*The princess was filled with **happiness. Happiness** was the main emotion she felt.*

Sometimes a yoked sentence can seem clumsy or contrived. In the examples opposite, a key word ends the first sentence and that **same** key word ends the second sentence, thereby elaborating or emphasising the meaning of the first. By this means, dual emphasis of the original point is achieved.

TEACHING TIPS AND GENRE LINKS

This sentence type can be used effectively in a wide range of genres as indicated in the given examples.

It is also useful for vocabulary development (generating and selecting the most effective key words for repetition) and extrapolation of ideas (for the content of the second sentence) as well as developing ways to emphasise points for different purposes - persuasion / creating tension / repetition to aid reader recall.

EXTENSION

Create a cliffhanger opening by adding a trailing-off sentence (see page 86) which negates the information given in the first two sentences to start a story as part of a flashback:

My brother and I did everything together. We grew, played and fought together. Then one day, all that came to a very unusual end...

I had it all sorted. Schoolwork, home life, it was all sorted. That was until my half-brother showed up and wrecked everything...

I ran. Oh, how I ran. Yet, the faster I went, the closer the beast seemed to get, until I could feel its hot breath on my neck...

FURTHER EXAMPLES

*Henry VIII was a man who displayed great **cruelty**. The lives of his wives, courtiers and opponents were all blighted by this **cruelty**.*
(Biographical recount)

*The main cause of the sinking of the Titanic was an **iceberg**. Some say that the speed she was travelling at was the critical factor, but speed would not have mattered without the **iceberg**.*

*The measurements of the universe are **vast**. Planet circumferences, distances between galaxies, all these numbers are staggeringly **vast**.*
(Explanation)

FIRST WORD LAST SENTENCES

7

EXAMPLES

*"**Brilliant**, the whole day was just **brilliant**!" Tilly beamed.*

*"**Rubbish**, the whole thing is a load of **rubbish**," Archer whispered.*
(Narrative)

*"**Madness**, this is **madness**!" declared the emissary as the Spartan leader threatened him with death.*
(Historical faction - combining fact and fiction)

EXPLANATION

Working on a similar premise to the previous sentence type, this sentence type opens with a key **first word** (usually an adjective derived from a character/authorial opinion)

"Brilliant,"

then continues by expanding upon that key word in a separate statement, which then ends with the same key word repeated last.

*"**Brilliant**, the whole day was just **brilliant**!"*

TEACHING TIPS AND GENRE LINKS

As can be seen from the examples this sentence is most useful in the context of dialogue. It can be used to teach reactive interjections that mirror speech, allowing insight into characters' opinions or simply allowing scope for clarification of those opinions via expansion and repetition.

EXTENSION

To vary the structure of the sentence in dialogue and avoid repetitive patterning, the position of the noun/verb combination (Archer whispered) can be moved,

*"Rubbish, the whole thing is a load of rubbish," **Archer whispered.***

*"Rubbish," **Archer whispered**, "the whole thing is a load of rubbish."*

***Archer whispered**, "Rubbish, the whole thing is a load of rubbish."*

A further variant would be to open with a verb,

Running, Sam never seemed to stop running.

Finally, you might introduce an ellipsis mark to convey a more dramatic mood.

Majestic...the alien panorama was truly majestic.

Shattered...with a few choice words, her trust was shattered.

INTERROBANG? SENTENCES

8

EXAMPLES

"Are you kidding me?" Sarah said in disbelief.

"Jack read a book? He's only three!" exclaimed Johnny as a look of jealousy spread slowly across his face.
(Narrative)

It was the sixth week at sea. "Haven't we reached our destination yet?" the crew bellowed, but Captain Bligh did not answer.
(Historical faction - linking fact and fiction)

EXPLANATION

Conceptualised in 1962 by American Martin K. Speckter, the head of an advertising agency, the interrobang combines the functions of the question mark (the "**interro**gative point") and the exclamation mark (known in printers' and programmers' terms as the "**bang**"). It is used when a question is asked in an excited or rhetorical manner, or when reactive excitement or disbelief is expressed as a question.

TEACHING TIPS AND GENRE LINKS

This sentence type is useful in the context of informal writing, particularly in direct speech, and could readily be linked to the *yoked sentence* (the last word of one sentence becomes the first word of the next sentence) as a means of introducing and explaining its use:

Mary knelt down and looked Steven gravely in the face. "Jack can't go with you. He's moving to Australia."

"Australia?" Steven replied in shock. "How could he? He's supposed to be my best friend!"

EXTENSION

Challenge pupils to research and apply other less frequently used punctuation marks, with the caveat that overusing them lessens their efficacy dramatically. They could consider:

Ditto mark (")

Asterisk (*)

Irony mark (؟)

Section break (***)

etc.

FURTHER EXAMPLES

James stood me up at the bus stop today. Can you believe it‽
(Diary entry)

"Is that hair flowing down from the window of that tower‽"
wondered the Prince as he rode up the hill.
(Fairytale)

"How could you betray me‽" Thor bellowed at his disloyal
brother Loki.
(Myth)

9 GETTING WORSE / GETTING BETTER SENTENCES

GETTING WORSE EXAMPLES

BAD   WORSE   EVEN WORSE

How would you feel if your child was **hurt**, **maimed** or **even killed** by a car?

Shouting out is **bad**, calling names is **worse**, but being violent is the **worst** thing anyone can do.

Wasting water is **damaging**, littering is even **more destructive**, but the **most catastrophic** environmental habit is producing air pollution with dirty engines.
(Persuasive)

We knew Tim was **naughty**, and his brother was **uncontrollable**, but their cousin Damien was **evil**.
(Narrative)

EXPLANATION

This sentence type serves to dramatically heighten a text and although it is commonly applied in persuasive texts, it is equally effective in the context of story writing.

Examples of 'Getting Worse Sentences' can be found opposite and examples of 'Getting Better Sentences' are overleaf.

TEACHING TIPS AND GENRE LINKS

This sentence type first appeared in *Teaching Outstanding Persuasive Writing (with 7-16 year olds)* by Alan Peat. It works well in persuasive writing, but it can also be used effectively in a range of other contexts.

It is best taught by taking a standard sentence and modelling how to turn it into a **Getting worse/better** sentence...

STANDARD SENTENCE

How would you feel if your child could be killed by a car?

SAME SENTENCE TURNED INTO A **GETTING WORSE** SENTENCE

How would you feel if your child could be hurt, maimed or even killed by a car?

Note that if the writer wishes to increase the dramatic tension even more, then the judicious use of an appropriate adjective toward the end of the sentence does help to achieve this aim. An example is provided below:

*How would you feel if your child could be hurt, maimed or even killed by a **speeding** car?*

Occasionally it is even possible to include two examples of dramatic heightening within the body of a single sentence.

EXAMPLE ONE *How would you feel if your child could be hurt, maimed or even killed by a...*

EXAMPLE TWO *...motorbike, car or **speeding** lorry?*

This sentence type is useful in grammatical terms for exploring comparative and superlative adjectives, as well as the use of rhetorical questions to engage the reader.

You could use word-generating competitions to create banks of alternative words for basic adjectives (good/bad) including comparatives and superlatives. It may be necessary to discuss when 'more' and 'most' are needed.

EXTENSION

Extend the application of this sentence type with **getting worse or better** verbs, and apply in the context of dialogue,

"You could have got lost, hurt, even killed! What were you thinking?" Aunt Sally demanded.

"Jack is a trouble maker, Jim is a thief, but must you hang around with John? He is a convicted criminal!" Billy's mum shouted.

A further variant would be to apply the technique described in the **Italics 'Stressed Word'** sentence type (see page 18).

"You could have got lost, hurt, even *killed*! What were you thinking?" Aunt Sally demanded.

"Jack is a trouble maker, Jim is a thief, but must you hang around with John? He is a *convicted criminal*!" Billy's mum shouted.

GETTING BETTER EXAMPLES

GOOD   BETTER   EVEN BETTER

*The best jokes make you **smile**, **giggle** or even **laugh out loud**!*

*Jack is **quick**, Mindy is even **faster**, but Holly is the **fastest** pupil in the whole class.*
(Report)

*Voltrex was **skilful**, Zanteng was a **master**, but the **most outstanding** lightphaser warrior by far was Jorten-Z*
(Narrative)

*Steam engines were **good**, combustion engines were even **better**, but hydrogen-powered engines are **set to change the world**.*
(Scientific report/Explanation)

10 DOES NOT / DOES (WILL NOT / WILL) SENTENCES

EXAMPLES

1. *I've known people who say that dropping a sweet wrapper **does not** matter. What **does** matter is the fact that if everyone thought like this then the world would be a dreadful place.*
(Persuasive writing)

2. *Some scientists have said that global warming **will not** negatively affect life on Earth. Others, however, are certain that it **will**. In this essay we will consider both sides of the debate.*
(Balanced argument)

3. *Some people say that humans **will not** be the dominant species on this planet forever. What **will happen** is that something will replace us. This is the story of the year of that replacement.*
(Narrative. Science fiction)

4. *David **does not** care about others. What he **does** care about is what he can get for himself.*
(Narrative)

5. *"No matter what happens, **I will not** fail!" Captain Rex pronounced. "What I **will** do is lead this crew to a glorious victory, in spite of the best efforts of cowardly General Slump."*
(Narrative)

EXPLANATION

Does not / does AND *Will not / will* sentences are another example of a double sentence and are often used when writing persuasively. Example 1 (opposite) would work well as the first two sentences of a persuasive essay which considers the negative impact of litter dropping.

When used persuasively, the information given in the second sentence negates the statement made in the initial sentence. In a sense, the first sentence is a presumption and the second is the reality. Put more simply, the first sentence is the opposite of the persuasive point the writer is actually making and the second sentence is the actual point of the persuasive piece.

This double sentence type works slightly differently if it is employed as the opening of a balanced argument (example 2). Used in this context the first sentence introduces one side of the argument and the second sentence introduces the opposing side of the same argument. It is a simple yet effective method of opening a balanced argument.

The third example demonstrates how this double sentence can be used to open a narrative flashback. If the two sentences in Example 3 were followed with a sentence such as,

It all began more or less a year ago...

then a flashback opening will have been successfully applied in the opening three sentences of the story.

TEACHING TIPS AND GENRE LINKS

Once again this sentence type is best taught through direct modelling and explicit discussion. We would recommend that if it is being used to open a text then the teacher also explicitly models how to continue writing after the double sentence opening. It is important to show pupils how to maintain the flow of their writing after using this double sentence - how to effectively transition from it into the remaining text.

As can be seen from the examples given, this is a flexible double sentence type which can be used across a broad range of genres.

EXTENSION

Challenge pupils to use a broader range of linking terms to widen potential application of the sentence, e.g.

cannot / can:

*We **cannot** all be professional footballers. What we **can** do is enjoy the game for its sportsmanship and camaraderie.*

should not / should:

*Some people think we **should not** concern ourselves so much with recycling. What we **should** realise is that planetary conservation is crucial, and recycling plays an enormous part.*

could not / could:

*Ben **could not** sing, or dance, or act. What he **could** do was write, and what an amazing writer he was.*

11 THEN AND NOW SENTENCES

EXAMPLES

1. *Months ago I used to eat meat, but now I am a vegetarian.*
(Persuasive)

2. *Although this was once a peaceful neighbourhood, now, with the building of the motorway, things are very different.*
(Persuasive)

3. *At first Wernher von Braun thought it was a normal assignment, but soon he realised it was something much more dangerous.*
(Report/Biographical recount)

EXPLANATION

The first part of this sentence opens with a time-related statement which describes the state of things as they were **then** (positive, negative or simply informative).

Months ago I used to eat meat,

The second part of the sentence usually presents an opposing perspective which describes how things are **now.**

Months ago I used to eat meat, but now I am a vegetation.

TEACHING TIPS AND GENRE LINKS

This sentence is very versatile, as shown in the examples. When teaching this sentence type we usually begin with a discussion of what was **THEN**, and what is **NOW**. This could be hypothetical (as in a persuasive starter: example 2, previous page), fictional, or even historical (as in example 3).

Once the two perspectives (what was and what is) have been established, a useful exercise is to think of pairs of linking words or phrases:

Years ago...but now...

Back then...today...

Even though...now it seems...

For a long time...until...

At first...but soon...

Although...now...

People once thought...however...

Not too long ago...now...

Initially...Now, however....

EXTENSION

Reduce the time period of the connecting terms to give a sense of urgency and alter mood quickly in a story while avoiding the 'suddenly...' pace shift that spoils a lot of writing:

__For a moment__, things seemed calm, __until__ they heard the unmistakable roar of the guardian dragon.

__One minute__ Jerry was right there; __the next__ he was snatched away into the shadows.

"__A second ago__ everything was fine; __now__ you're telling me we have to evacuate! What is going on?" Jane screamed.

FURTHER EXAMPLES

Many years ago when I visited the museum it seemed dull, but today, I confess, I loved it!
(Diary)

In the 1890s opportunities to travel were limited for most people, though today many of us take even flights between continents for granted.
(Comparison contrast report)

Once, all the animals in Dingle Wood lived in harmony, but since the vicious wolfpack arrived, things have been very different indeed.
(Folktale)

SUBJECT - 3 EXAMPLES - ARE ALL SENTENCES

12

EXAMPLES

My favourite animals - lions, tigers and sharks - are all owners of very sharp teeth!

Cosmic events - shooting stars, eclipses and auroras - are all infrequent and impressive in equal measure.
(Report)

Extreme sports - motocross, BASE jumping and white-water rafting - are all equally dangerous!
(Persuasive or Report)

EXPLANATION

This is an example of a three-part sentence. The **subject** opens the sentence, followed by three **examples** of the subject (with a dash before and a dash after). Finally, a common feature of the three examples concludes the sentence, which is introduced by the words **are all**.

TEACHING TIPS AND GENRE LINKS

One engaging way to generate these sentences is to provide the **examples** and ask the pupils to extrapolate the **subject** and '**are all**' parts of the sentence using the questions 'What are they?' and 'What links them?'

For example:

Examples (Vocabulary linked to the target topic/research area) = tuk-tuks, gondolas and trams
What are they? = vehicles from around the world
What links them? = they are used as public transport
Sentence = *Many different vehicles - like tuk-tuks, gondolas and trams - are used as public transport around the world.*

Examples (Vocabulary linked to the target topic/research area) = Catherine of Aragon, Anne Boleyn, Catherine Howard and Jane Seymour
What are they? = Four of Henry VIII's wives
What links them? They died during Henry's reign
Sentence = *Four of Henry VIII's wives - Catherine of Aragon, Anne Boleyn, Catherine Howard and Jane Seymour - died during his reign.*

Examples (Vocabulary linked to the target topic/research area) = exercise, clean living and a balanced diet
What are they? = healthy habits
What links them? = they help to maximise lifespan
Sentence = *Developing healthy habits - exercise, clean living and a balanced diet - can help to maximise your lifespan.*

After this, consider providing the pupils with a range of subjects (the first third of the sentence) and ask them to complete the following two thirds in an interesting manner.

To avoid decontextualised drilling, some examples could be chosen for a wall display which would then become a useful visual referent for future writing.

EXTENSION

Adapt for narrative and combine with other sentence types as a story starter and an engaging way of introducing a character or a setting:

The Draven boy - odd, eccentric and creepy - only moved into town a week ago, yet everyone seemed to think it was best to stay away from him...
(Combined with a Trailing off sentence)

The old abandoned coal mine - dark, dangerous and remote - was the last place anyone would want to find themselves on a cold, stormy winter's night...
(Combined with 2A and *Trailing off* sentence)

FURTHER EXAMPLES

My favourite drinks - Coke, Fanta and Tizer - are all fizzy.
(Report)

Parties - with friends, colleagues or even people I've never met before - are all just as traumatic for me.
(Diary or First Person narrative)

Fires - bonfires, gas rings or matches - are all equally dangerous!
(Explanation: in this instance an explanation of fire hazards and fire safety)

WHEN_ ; WHEN_ ; WHEN_ , THEN_. SENTENCES

13

EXAMPLES

When tumultuous thunder shakes the ground; when blinding lightning tears the sky; when storm clouds block every ray of hopeful light, then you know the Kraken is approaching.
(Narrative - using weather to create a specific mood)

When you look at the remains of Tutankhamen; when you examine the damage to his skull; when you look at the motives of his advisors, then it is clear that the young Pharaoh's death should be treated as suspicious.
(Historical report)

When the air around you suddenly freezes; when your blood chills; when the sudden silence terrifies you, then the haunting begins.
(Ghost story)

When the transponders rattle with static; when the mothership fades from sight; when the blood-red moon rises, then you know you are all alone on the hostile planet.
(Science fiction)

When the Queen gives birth to her first son; when the wise women of the Kingdom rejoice; when the streets echo with the sound of joyful laughter, then you know that Evil has finally been banished.
(Fairy tale)

EXPLANATION

This sentence type ends with a statement e.g.

...the haunting begins.

This concluding statement is preceded by three examples of occurrences which, when combined, lend credibility/prove/ predict the final statement.

This sentence is often employed as a visually striking paragraph (or story opening).

TEACHING TIPS AND GENRE LINKS

We would strongly suggest that this sentence type is best taught IN REVERSE e.g. starting with the concluding statement and 'working backwards'.

In class this would occur in the following way...

Teacher:

"We are going to write a *When; when; when; then* sentence together. I'm going to give you the end of the sentence...(writes on whiteboard *...then the haunting begins*). Can you think of three things which might happen in the haunted house to prove that the haunting has begun?"

Discuss the effect of leading with the word **'when'** (use of 'when' invites the 'then' - hooking the reader in - even better when directly addressing the reader). Start with the **'then'** and work backwards to establish the signs of the event.

Event: a bad holiday

Signs: lost luggage, late trains, broken bed

Combined into a When_; when_; when_, then_.

When the luggage gets lost; when the trains are delayed; when the bed in the hotel is broken, then the holiday isn't going to go well.

Pupils would then suggest ideas and the teacher would model how to use these to produce the sentence type.

The sentence also provides a useful teaching link to the use of semicolons in an extended list.

EXTENSION

Use the same process and increase the complexity of the events:

Fiction example:

Event - an alien invasion
Signs - UFO sightings, abductions, electrical disturbances

Combined into a When_; when_; when_, then_.

When strange objects are spotted flying through the sky; when people begin to disappear mysteriously; when strange images distort your TV screen, then you'd better prepare for an alien invasion.

Non-fiction example:

Event: dragonfly emerging
Signs: nymph stage completed, larva emerges on plants, metamorphosis takes places,

Combined into a When_; when_; when_, then_.

When the nymph has grown to the larval stage; when the creature has found a reed to climb; when the metamorphosis takes place, then you will see the rebirth of an amazingly beautiful creature.

Another useful extension/variant would be the *It was; it was; it was - in short* sentence. Dickens uses a (very long!) example of this at the start of 'A Tale of Two Cities',

It was the best of times, it was the worst of times, it was the age of wisdom, it was the age of foolishness, it was the epoch of belief, it was the epoch of incredulity, it was the season of Light, it was the season of Darkness, it was the spring of hope, it was the winter of despair...

(Note: Dickens could have used semicolons!)

14 ADVERB FROM ADJECTIVE SENTENCES

EXAMPLES

*He was a **horrible** person, in fact he acted **horribly** all the time.*
(Narrative: simple example)

*The tyrant king was **brutal**, and he dealt with disloyal subjects **brutally**.*
(Historical report/Biographical recount)

*They said he was **vicious**, and he certainly treated his poor dog **viciously**.*
(Narrative: character description)

EXPLANATION

This is a two-part sentence. The first part is a descriptive statement which includes an adjective.

*He was a **sad** man*

The second part of the sentence adds further detail, usually in the form of a related action, which utilises an adverb directly derived from the adjective in the first part of the sentence.

*walking **sadly** down the road.*

TEACHING TIPS AND GENRE LINKS

This sentence type lends itself most readily to the narrative genre. It is a pithy sentence type which helps pupils to understand how adverbs of manner function.

A key point to discuss with pupils is the placing of the adverb as this can radically alter the meaning of the sentence.

*He was a **sad** man, walking **sadly** down the street*

(= the man was walking sadly)

*He was a **sad** man, **sadly** walking down the street*

(This could imply that the narrator is sad that he is walking down the street, or it could be an error on the part of the writer - split infinitive)

This sentence once again reinforces the idea that actions should be informed by characteristics, and it is also useful when teaching subordinate and main clauses, and the '**and**' connective.

When introducing this sentence type it may be useful to begin with an example sentence and examine a range of possible adjective/adverb combinations.

The person was_____ and they acted _____

generous - generously

cold - coldly

brave - bravely

selfish - selfishly

dishonest - dishonestly

delightful - delightfully

EXTENSION

Vary focus (which thus far has been character-based) to include locational writing.

*It was a **spooky** place - even the branches of the trees moved **spookily**.*

(Narrative: locational writing)

FURTHER EXAMPLES

It was a violent crime and when the mob caught the perpetrator he was beaten violently.
(Newspaper report)

Florence Nightingale was famed for being compassionate, and she treated each and every one of her patients compassionately.
(Biographical recount)

Recycling is easy, and this explanation will demonstrate just how easily you can recycle in your own home.
(Explanation of a process)

DESCRIPTION, WHICH + SIMIL SENTENCES

EXAMPLES

Greg had huge nostrils, which made him look like a hippo.

Doctor Swogflop bathed only once a year, which meant he was as smelly as a skunk's bottom most of the time!
(Narrative)

The valleys have crooked ravines, which curve around like the blade of a scimitar.
(Geographical report or explanation)

EXPLANATION

This is a two-part sentence. A **simile** is employed in the second part which elaborates on the **description** presented in the first part.

TEACHING TIPS AND GENRE LINKS

Use vivid descriptions to generate a simile by first thinking about the effect / mood which the description engenders:

Doctor Swogflop bathed only once a year.
Effect = to have the reader imagine his smell.

Then, using the identified quality, generate an appropriate simile:

, which meant he was as smelly as a skunk's bottom most of the time.

Remind pupils that the most effective similes compare the subject to something that it is different from in as many ways as possible, except for the desired comparative quality i.e. the simile

, which meant he smelled as bad as a sweaty footballer.

is not as effective as

, which meant he smelled as bad as a sweaty footballer's unwashed sock.

This sentence is also useful for teaching the *which* connective in clauses.

EXTENSION

Begin by exploring the differences between similes and metaphors, discussing how examples might be converted from one to the other. Next, generate a variety of metaphorical comparisons which follow the *description, which + simile* pattern. Include a dash before the metaphor so that pupils grasp both techniques:

The valleys have crooked ravines - the scars of a giant's dagger.

The valleys have crooked ravines - the veins of the earth.

The valleys have crooked ravines - the pathways of time.

Greg had huge nostrils - he was a walking, talking hippo.

Greg had huge nostrils - hoovers protruding from his face.

Greg had huge nostrils - black holes that disappeared into his empty head.

THIS IS THAT SENTENCES

EXAMPLES

His eyes were dark tunnels.
(Narrative: character description)

The lake was a mirror.
(Narrative: location description)

The explorers knew they were standing on the shoulders of giants.
(Report)

EXPLANATION

This sentence is an example of a metaphor: a figure of speech that describes a subject by stating that it is, by way of a point of comparison, the same as another otherwise unrelated object.

TEACHING TIPS AND GENRE LINKS

Metaphors are often a difficult figure of speech for pupils to grasp. Although a simile is relatively straightforward, the idea that something IS (by point of comparison) the SAME as something entirely different is a cognitively sophisticated concept.

The concept of metaphors should not, therefore, be taught until the concept of a simile is fully grasped.

Once pupils understand, and have successfully used similes in their writing, then metaphors can be discussed. It is always best to do this using modelled examples.

As in the previous sentence type, it is useful to discuss how the comparative image is often most effective when it reflects the quality of the subject in a **single** way, and is as different from the subject in all other ways as possible. Therefore, the identification of the desired quality is key when creating a metaphor.

One way to do this is to brainstorm ideas based on the desired/key quality, i.e. if the key quality of the man's eyes in the first example is that they are especially **dark**, you might ask, *What kind of things are dark?* to which you may get suggestions like:

The night sky

My bedroom

A dungeon

A coal mine

The grave

A tunnel

A cave

A cellar

Death

Select the most effective ideas (those which most readily relate to the identified quality, but which are different in as many other ways as possible) and demonstrate how they might be employed in a **this is that** manner:

His eyes were dark tunnels.

His eyes were pitch-black cellars.

His eyes were dank caves.

His eyes were empty graves.

Metaphors are most readily suited to the narrative genre, but they can be used successfully in other contexts such as persuasive writing.

EXTENSION

Replace the full stop at the end of the metaphor with the connective *which*, followed by further information which extends the metaphor.

His eyes were dark tunnels which led to his darker soul.

His eyes were pitch-black cellars which held years of lost secrets.

His eyes were dank caves which you dared not venture too far into.

17 WHAT + ! SENTENCES

EXAMPLES

What a lovely day!
(Really pleased)

What a truly ghastly sight!
(Really disgusted)

What a tragic event!
(Really upset)

What an innovative design!
(Really impressed)

EXPLANATION

Once again this is a three-part sentence. It always begins with the word 'What', which is then followed by an adjective which describes the final word/s of the sentence, those being its subject.

What a lovely day!
    Adjective Subject

The sentence always concludes with an exclamation mark which indicates that a strong emotion (either negative or positive) is involved.

TEACHING TIPS AND GENRE LINKS

We would suggest that, since the exclamation mark is an essential feature of this sentence type, the What+! sentence provides an ideal opportunity to revisit the broad range of situations in which exclamation marks are used. (See 'Get Your Head Around Punctuation' by Alan Peat, Creative Educational Press Ltd p. 29.)

An Alphabet of both positive and negative adjectives (Amazing, Brilliant, Catastrophic...) can be turned into a poster to help to broaden the range of adjectives used by pupils. To ensure that the display is both cumulative and collaborative, a felt marker should be left beneath the poster and pupils should be encouraged to add other appropriate adjectives which they find when reading, either in school or at home.

If all staff use the word 'Really' when explaining this sentence type, then the concept of linking exclamation marks to sentences which convey strong emotion will more readily be grasped.

What a great game! = REALLY happy.

What a vile thing! = REALLY disgusted.

The sentence type works well in the context of dialogue when one character reacts to a previous character's utterance...

"We need to split up. We'll find them faster that way," Greg suggested.

"What a terrible idea!" James snapped. "We'd be just as lost in no time!"

...or to a prior event:

As the exploration crew reached the highest ridge of the mountain, the whole vista came into view. "What an incredible sight!" exclaimed Captain Riggs as he surveyed the landscape that lay sprawled out before him.

A fun way to generate these statements is to ask pupils to adopt the persona of a character in your focal story or topic. Provide them with a scenario in which they find themselves, and then ask them to produce a reaction freeze (a still, dramatic posture) and to have one thought in their minds. Next, go round the group with a microphone and as you record them, they must voice their reaction in the form of a **What+!** Sentence. Encourage pupils to use all of their senses.

For example, you may ask pupils to imagine they are Charlie, entering Willy Wonka's factory for the first time, and you may get responses like:

"What an extraordinary building!"

"What a delicious smell!"

"What an odd creature!"

"What an awful din!"

This sentence type is best suited to the narrative genre and playscripts, though it can also be useful in persuasive adverts.

EXTENSION

Adapt the **What+!** sentence as a means of revealing the inner thoughts of a character by altering the verb that follows the **What+!** sentence.

"What an incredible sight!" **exclaimed** *Captain Riggs as he surveyed the landscape that lay sprawled out before him.*

becomes

"What an incredible sight!" **thought** *Captain Riggs as he surveyed the landscape that lay sprawled out before him.*

This psychological window can be easily extended, and the authorial voice exercised to put the reader in a 'knowing' position, by adding a trailing off sentence (see page 86).

"What an incredible sight!" thought Captain Riggs as he surveyed the landscape that lay sprawled out before him. **Little did he know that in less than 24 hours, his whole world would be turned upside down...**

EDS AND INGS SENTENCES

18

ED, ING, ED EXAMPLES

*The rabbit **turned** towards the log, **sniffing** the air, then it **hopped** on top.*

*Jack **dragged** himself up from the pavement, **hurling** insults, and **raced** after the robber.*
(Narrative)

*Newton **jumped** up, **dusting** himself off, and **picked** up the fallen apple.*
(Historical faction)

EXPLANATION

This sentence is a development of the original '**ing, ed**' (see *Writing Exciting Sentences* page 55), and is actually a sequence or pattern of verbs (past tense **eds** and present participle **ings**) that enable the writer to convey simultaneous or sequential action for dramatic impact.

TEACHING TIPS AND GENRE LINKS

The patterns demonstrated above are just two possible arrangements. For example, you could begin with a simple **ed, ing** form:

*Jack **jumped** on his bike and went **speeding** down the street.*

Or an **ed, ed, ing**:

*Tracy **blinked** and **rubbed** her eyes, **refusing** to believe what she saw.*

Or an **ing, ing, ed**!:

***Tossing** and **turning** in bed, the soldier **launched** his pillow across the room at the sudden noise of the alarm.*

As more forms are introduced, assigning individual names for each variation may become counterproductive. Instead, focus on the selection of appropriate simultaneous or sequential actions which correspond to the correct word endings. This also offers an opportunity to consider correct comma and connective usage.

Due to their sequential nature, comics are an effective resource, as pupils can be challenged to condense the actions of two or three 'cells' into a single sentence. **(see *Developing Writing Through Comics* by Mathew Sullivan, Creative Educational Press Ltd)**

EXTENSION

Enhance these sentences with appropriately placed adverbs. For example:

The rabbit turned towards the log, sniffing the air **cautiously**, *then it hopped on top.*

Jack dragged himself up from the pavement, hurling insults, and raced **frantically** *after the robber.*

Jack jumped on his bike **excitedly** *and went speeding down the street.*

Tossing and turning **violently** *in bed, the soldier launched his pillow across the room at the sudden noise of the alarm.*

ING, ING, ING EXAMPLES

Hopping, skipping, jumping, *he made his way to the park.*

Shaking, trembling, quaking, *he walked further into the blackness.*
(Narrative)

Stomping, screaming, shaking, *King Henry ordered the execution of his latest wife.*
(Historical faction)

19 MOST IMPORTANT - IN SHORT SENTENCES

EXAMPLES

Above all *the sea is feared by many for the distance it places sailors from safety -* ***in short****, it is a vast and often dangerous place.*
(Report)

Jack took children's lunch treats, pushed people over in the playground and shouted at just about anyone - in short, Jack was not a pleasant boy.
(Narrative: simple negative characterisation)

The engine was shot, two tyres had punctures and every window was shattered - in short, the vehicle was useless to the stranded crew.
(Narrative: conveying peril)

But above all the debate about whether fox-hunting should be banned or not will run and run - in short, everyone has strong opinions on the matter.
(Balanced argument)

But above all fox-hunting should be banned because of the extreme cruelty involved in the chase and the kill - in short, it is barbaric.
(Persuasive)

EXPLANATION

Although this is a complex sentence type, it is quite readily grasped by more able children. This sentence type is typically employed at the conclusion of several previous sentences on a subject. It states several of the most (or one of the most) important aspects of the subject then ends (after the words **in short**) with the same thing stated more pithily. Essentially the end of the sentence is summative.

TEACHING TIPS AND GENRE LINKS

This sentence type is useful across a wide range of genres as the examples given demonstrate. In cross-curricular literacy, history provides an ideal vehicle for discussing this sentence type and this is how we have most often taught it.

Pupils read a range of texts / source materials about a character and after reading, select three key aspects of that person's character and ONE word or phrase which best sums them up e.g.

CHURCHILL

3 key aspects of character: inspirational, dogged, tireless

ONE word or phrase that best sums him up: a leader

This is then turned into the sentence e.g.

Above all he was inspirational, dogged and tireless - in short, a leader!

The second part of the sentence helps pupils to develop their ability to carefully select vocabulary, as they are essentially challenged to repeat the same information in a new way (helping them to adapt, summarise and conclude).

EXTENSION

Extend this sentence by adding a BOYS sentence after it (one which contains **b**ut, **o**r, **y**et or **s**o). The BOYS sentence negates or modifies the perspective established in the first sentence. Finally, conclude by **trailing off** (page 86) thereby creating an engaging story opener.

The engine was shot, two tyres had punctures and every window was shattered - in short, the vehicle was useless to the stranded crew. **But** *this was about to become the least of their worries...*

The sea is feared by many owing to its unpredictable behaviour and the distance it places sailors from safety - in short, it is a vast, dangerous place. **Yet** *this did not deter Captain J. Rickshaw as he set off from the harbour towards the Bermuda Triangle...*

FURTHER EXAMPLES

But above all he was a man for whom wealth and success came easily - in short, he was perfectly suited for the Victorian era.
(Narrative: positive characterisation)

He was a man to whom cruelty, greed and ruthlessness came easily - in short, he was evil.
(Narrative : negative characterisation)

But above all it was a house with a calming, relaxed atmosphere - in short, it was a home.
(Narrative: locational writing)

Henry VIII is remembered for his ruthlessness, stubbornness and apparent heartlessness - in short, he was a tyrant.
(Biographical Recount)

TRAILING OFF... SENTENCES

20

EXAMPLES

1. The Trojans pulled the wooden horse inside their walls and retired for a peaceful sleep...
(Historical fiction: a dramatic pause or the beginning of a flashback)

2. He smiled, took her hand and led her away from the house...
(End of a narrative. This conclusion leaves the rest to the reader's imagination.)

3. "I watched my husband fall, the second bullet struck him and then..."
(Narrative: overcome by negative emotion)

EXPLANATION

This sentence type is deliberately unfinished. An essential part of this sentence type is the ellipsis mark which is used to indicate that something is missing - the end of the sentence.

In example 1 what is missing is the rest of the story. The sentence trails off.

In example 2 what is missing is a concluding statement. The sentence trails off before the final action is described, thereby leaving it to the reader's imagination.

In example 3 the dialogue trails off because the speaker is overcome with emotion and cannot continue.

In all of the examples provided, the technique allows the reader an insight into the future development of the narrative e.g. the words *until* and *or so they thought* both indicate that something contrary to expectation is about to occur. This is an important aspect of the sentence type: it either requires the reader to 'fill gaps' (examples 2 and 3) or it places the reader in a more knowledgable position than the characters (example 1).

TEACHING TIPS AND GENRE LINKS

This sentence type is most suited to playscripts and narrative writing. It is best taught using modelled examples as points for discussion. We recommend that, when using this sentence type to begin a flashback, the kind of bridging sentences which follow the *Trailing off...* sentence are also explored e.g.

Everything was fine until...

Well, I guess I may be jumping ahead of myself. Let's go back to the very beginning.

When this sentence type is used in the context of a playscript it is usually accompanied by a stage direction e.g.

Barbara: (Choking back tears) The last time I saw him was when he...

Note that we have seen *Trailing off* sentences used by pupils as a way of prematurely ending a story they are not enjoying writing. This is clearly not an appropriate use of the sentence type! Provide a bank of *Trailing off* phrases to give pupils a clearer idea of effective usage:

But that wasn't the case...

That was until...

Everything seemed fine, however...

Everyone thought they were OK...

Or so they...

But all wasn't as it seemed...

They thought...

EXTENSION

Combine this sentence type with the *Sound! Cause* (page 102) sentence to create an exciting dramatic link between two paragraphs:

"We've made it!" Jack mouthed silently as the last of the soldiers squeezed into the disused bomb shelter. **The giants would never find them in there, or so he thought...**

CRACK! The floor of the shelter tore wide open and an immense, gnarled hand grabbed two of the soldiers and pulled them down into the darkness. *The giants had tunnelled underground!*

FURTHER EXAMPLES

The only warning the people of the outlying villages near Hiroshima got was a flash of light. That was until...
(Historical faction - linking fact and fiction)

The car sped over the ledge toward the rocks below...
(Flashback - first sentence of the story)

I just can't believe...
(Narrative: overcome by emotion - either negative or positive)

SO...
SENTENCES

21

EXAMPLES

He'd never felt so...odd.

Max disappearing the same day the big lottery win was announced? It was just so...strange.
(Narrative)

Howard Carter could not believe what he had discovered. It was just so...astounding.
(Historical faction)

EXPLANATION

This sentence is similar to the previous one in its use of the ellipsis mark to create tension. Now, however, it is also used to indicate a character's struggle to 'get a handle' on the moment or gain an understanding of an emotion or event. It works by identifying an overwhelming feeling and placing it after the ellipsis.

TEACHING TIPS AND GENRE LINKS

This sentence type works well as an aspect of effective characterisation. It is useful when demonstrating conflicting emotions and it allows the writer to include a lesser-used punctuation mark when alluding to characters' thought processes. It is also useful when conveying confusion and disbelief after a striking statement.

Introduce this sentence type using the following statements and work out endings with pupils:

Everyone had left him. He'd never felt so...

He had nothing, then suddenly he was a millionaire! It was all so...

The scientist could not believe what he was seeing. It was so...

You might then create your own sentence starters based on your focal text and challenge pupils to conclude them.

EXTENSION

This sentence type could be an effective stepping-stone to a technique introduced in the *Developing Writing Through Comics* book called 'tag questions for uncertainty' which also uses the ellipsis mark to convey uncertainty and tension,

This couldn't be real...could it?

"He will save us...won't he?"

FURTHER EXAMPLES

I had never seen something so... terrible.
(Diary)

The alien technology was so... mindblowing!
(Science fiction)

The Princess was so... incredibly beautiful.
(Fairytale)

SINGLE WORD SENTENCES

22

EXAMPLES

No. Yes. Fine. Right! Well! Then... So... So? And? Pardon? What? Never! Really? Seriously? Hmm... Who? What? When? Where? Why? How? Sometimes. Maybe. Excellent! Brilliant! Classy! Oh. Stay. Go! Precisely. Definitely. Unquestionably. Guess! Anytime! Cool! Rubbish! Stop! Please! Hey! Certainly. Absolutely. Always! Occasionally. Rarely. Quickly! Slowly! Quietly! Wait. Walk. Run! Impossible! Boring! Great! Fine! Amazing! Yes!

EXPLANATION

As we don't wish to receive a barrage of pedantic emails and letters, let's be clear that we do understand that if one takes the standard grammatical definition of a sentence, then a sentence needs to contain a subject and a verb. Let's also be clear that the examples opposite don't (though some have an implied subject). So if you prefer, call it a statement.

You will find these one-word statements/sentences in many, many books by a huge range of authors, and as their publishing houses (and editors) deemed it perfectly acceptable and didn't edit them out of the finished texts, we're more than happy to include them in this book.

Happy?

Fantastic!

Unhappy?

Tough!

TEACHING TIPS AND GENRE LINKS

The most sensible way to teach this is to draw pupils' attention to examples in both shared and guided reading. Sometimes the single word is an elliptical version of a longer sentence. This occurs most often in dialogue when both speakers clearly know what the subject of their conversation is and so have no need to repeat it in every spoken sentence. It also occurs when the meaning is obvious as a result of previous dialogue. This is best explained by example,

"Should we go home at the usual time?"

"Usual?"

One word (Usual) replaces,

"Remind me what the usual time is?"

The meaning is clear - there is no need for the overly verbose sentence which bears no relation to how we actually speak.

Amazing!

EXTENSION

Try asking pupils to play verbal 'Word Keepy Up' in pairs. An example is provided below:

Hi

OK?

Yes.

Good.

You?

Tired.

Why?

School.

Yawn!

Exactly!

Plans?

TV?

No.

X-box?

Sure!

OK.

23 EMOTION - CONSEQUENCE SENTENCES

EXAMPLES

David was angry - he threw his toy at the wall.

The professor was inconsolable - he wept for days on end.
(Narrative)

King Henry was furious - he ordered the execution of his wife.
(Historical report or Biographical recount)

EXPLANATION

This two-part sentence starts with a description of a character's **emotion**:

*David was **angry***

followed by a dash and a description of a **consequence** of that feeling:

*David was angry - **he threw his toy at the wall.***

TEACHING TIPS AND GENRE LINKS

Again, this sentence relates to the idea of characteristics informing actions – a subject which is examined in more detail in the *Developing Writing Through Comics* book.

It could be taught in a cross-curricular manner during PSHE, particularly through drama, when looking at emotions and their consequences. This would easily transfer into an exploration of character empathy - looking at how a character would feel (considering aspects of their personality and their social context), and as a result, what they might do.

This sentence also facilitates a teaching opportunity regarding the function of the dash in a sentence.

EXTENSION

Change the ending to refer to both the past (hinting at a reason for the emotion) and the future (a prediction of what the emotion is going to make the character do.)

Past - *Kevin was devastated - he'd **been** working on that project for five long years.*

Future - *Eric was furious - he **started** to plot his vengeance.*

FURTHER EXAMPLES

Romeo was dumbfounded - he'd never seen such beauty until that night.
(Romantic fiction)

The killer was crazed - he washed his hands in the dripping blood.
(Horror)

Captain Smith was determined - he continued through the ice despite the warning telegraphs.
(Historical report - sinking of the Titanic)

24 SOUND! CAUSE SENTENCES

EXAMPLES

Splat! The water balloon burst as it hit the wall.

Bang! The lift exploded as it reached the ground floor, covering the hallway in thick smoke.
(Narrative)

Whump! Another sandstone block fell into place. The pyramid was beginning to take shape.
(Historical faction)

EXPLANATION

This sentence opens with an attention-grabbing **sound** word, and then unfolds with an explanation of what **caused** the sound. It is useful when developing an understanding of onomatopoeic words, a concept expanded upon in the *Developing Writing Through Comics* book.

TEACHING TIPS AND GENRE LINKS

When focusing on this we suggest that the teacher introduces this sentence type using common onomatopoeic terms (bang, smash, crash, crack, wallop, smack, etc.) then extends to more abstract ones (flump, whump, blip, etc.). Each time, the teacher should provide the pupils with the onomatopoeic word before exploring the range of actions which may have caused that sound. Once pupils are confident, encourage them to think about the action before selecting an appropriate onomatopoeic word.

EXTENSION

If a suitable onomatopoeic word doesn't exist - create one (a neologism)! Comics may be useful for this as they are littered with 'made up' sound words. Some onomatopoeic words first coined in comics have become well-known in their own right (such as the 'snikt', which occurs when Wolverine's claws pop out!).

FURTHER EXAMPLES

Bang! DarkSpectre landed heavily on the groaning metal walkway, intent on stopping the psychotic criminal.
(Comic strip)

Zap! The warp phaser propelled the Hypership into a slingshot orbit around the planet.
(Science fiction)

C-r-e-a-k! The floorboards slowly began to tear themselves apart, revealing the mummified body.
(Ghost story)

25 WITH A(N) ACTION, MORE ACTION SENTENCES

EXAMPLES

With a smile, Greg waved goodbye.
(Narrative)

With a weary wail, Thor launched his final attack.
(Narrative or Historical faction)

With a deep breath, Neil Armstrong stepped carefully on to the surface of the moon.
(Recent historical faction)

EXPLANATION

This two-part sentence begins with a subordinate clause which starts with the phrase '**With a(n)**', followed by an **action** and a **comma**:

With a weary wail,

The main clause then describes **more action** which occurs simultaneously (this could be thought of as the 'main action'):

With a weary wail, Thor launched his final attack.

TEACHING TIPS AND GENRE LINKS

These sentences, like the **ed, ing** sentences, are useful when teaching pupils how to describe simultaneous actions, helping them to avoid descriptions of a succession of single, seemingly unrelated events.

You can demonstrate the idea of simultaneous actions easily in class - you will be doing it without even thinking! As you speak your hands are moving, you are looking around, you are listening for questions etc. Take one of these simple actions and discuss what could be happening simultaneously. Extend this process to a focal text and let suggestions be informed by the narrative context:

Context - *trying to open a treasure chest*

Action? - *picking up a lost key*

And at the same time? - *sighing with relief*

Combined - *With a sigh of relief, I picked up the lost key.*

This sentence type is also useful when teaching main and subordinate clauses and their related punctuation.

EXTENSION

Triple the action by including an 'as' clause at the end.

*With a weary wail, Thor launched his final attack **as his enemies scattered helplessly.***

FURTHER EXAMPLES

With a sigh of distress, I left him at the station.
(Diary)

With an air of absolute confidence, Winston Churchill approached the microphone.
(Diary or First Person narrative)

With a final dash of pepper, the dish will be ready to serve.
(Instructional genre: final sentence of a recipe)

26 POSITION + PLACE, SUBJECT + ACTION SENTENCES

EXAMPLES

At the top of the tallest tree, the monkey sat and gobbled down the banana.

High up above the ruined skyscrapers, Jess could see clouds of giant insects swarming across the sky.
(Narrative)

Deep beneath the choppy waves, the torpedo moved silently towards its target.
(Historical faction or narrative)

EXPLANATION

Another two-part sentence: it opens with a subordinate clause which describes the **position + place** of the action in specific terms (i.e. not just the 'where', but a more specific location within the where) e.g.

High up above the **ruined skyscrapers**,

Position   Place

The main clause which follows opens with a naming of the **subject**, followed by an appropriate description of an **action**:

High up above the ruined skyscrapers, **Jess could see** *clouds of giant insects swarming across the sky.*

TEACHING TIPS AND GENRE LINKS

As can be seen from the examples, this is a versatile sentence type which can be used to describe the actions of people, animals or objects. It is also useful when exploring positional language and the use of dependent clauses.

Finally, it encourages pupils to think about where they are specifically in a setting.

You might explore this by providing images of a variety of locations and asking children where they could situate a character specifically (use a 'pin the tail' game with a blu-tacked character on a whiteboard setting display - challenge children to write a **Position + place, subject + action** sentence based on the character's final location.)

EXTENSION

Use a verb to start the sentence which suggests *how* the character is interacting with the setting, before their actions are described and clarified in the second clause:

Spying *from the depths of the bunker, Jade began to tunnel her way towards the secret base.*

FURTHER EXAMPLES

In the centre of many towns, children sit in fast-food outlets consuming copious amounts of saturated fats. In this essay we will demonstrate how dangerous this habit is.
(Persuasive genre: opening paragraph)

At the top of the Wellington Arch, I looked out to see the Horse Guards approaching.
(Recount - of a trip to London)

In the deep, dark shadows of the bridge a Troll crouched, sharpening his teeth.
(Fairytale)

ACTION AS IF SENTENCES

EXAMPLES

The boy cried and screamed as if that would change his mother's mind.

William stared intently at the clock as if it would make the hands turn faster.
(Narrative)

Pilate washed his hands as if ridding himself of all responsibilities.
(Religious faction)

EXPLANATION

This sentence opens with a description of an **action**, which is usually quite intense in nature.

The boy cried and screamed

This is followed by the words '**as if**', then a description of the character's intent, which serves to explain the action and provides an insight into their motivations and desires.

The boy cried and screamed as if that would change his mother's mind.

TEACHING TIPS AND GENRE LINKS

When teaching this sentence type it would perhaps be useful to work backwards: generate the end of the sentence first, and the gesture afterward e.g.

Teacher: What is it your characters want?

Pupil: To win the race

Teacher: What actions would they take to do that?

Pupil: Tie laces tighter, stare at opponents, look at the crowd, pump their legs and arms etc.

Teacher: Now pick one of those and combine it with what you said your character wanted, using the words 'as if':

Megan tied her shoes as tightly as possible as if that would help her win the race.

EXTENSION

Make the subject of the sentence an inanimate object or natural feature and use this to explore personification...

The factory walls groaned and shook as if their workload was too much to take.

...or pathetic fallacy,

The wind lashed wildly and violently around the house as if it knew how terrified the occupants were.

FURTHER EXAMPLES

You talk about the construction of this road as if it will have no impact on the lives of locals.
(Formal letter of complaint)

The Superhero pleaded with the desperate villain as if it would stop his dreadful plan.
(Comic strip)

The crew member smashed the control panel with a wrench as if it would solve the problem of the broken thruster.
(Science fiction)

28 AS _LY SENTENCES

EXAMPLES

As the rain came down heavily, the children ran for shelter.

As the wind screamed wildly through the blackened trees, the lost giant lumbered along the path.
(Narrative)

As the water heats up quickly, a change of state happens called 'evaporation'.
(Explanation)

EXPLANATION

This sentence provides another way of conveying simultaneous actions, with a particular focus on *how* those actions are related. It opens with an action description which starts with the word '**As**' and ends with an adverb (**_ly** word) and a comma:

As *the rain came down* **heavily**,

It then proceeds with a description of a related, and often consequential, action:

As the rain came down heavily, **the children ran for shelter.**

TEACHING TIPS AND GENRE LINKS

This sentence type is particularly useful when conveying the importance and usefulness of the word 'as' (in this context meaning 'occurring at the same time' rather than 'like' - the use that more pupils will be familiar with through simile work).

It is also useful for teaching pupils about adverbs (referred to as 'words ending in ly' thereby avoiding metalanguage-based confusion) and related clauses.

EXTENSION

Invert the order of the sentence to put the 'as' phrase second, so that pupils have access to greater structural variety.

As he stared blankly at the test in front of him, Peter chewed the end of his pencil.

becomes:

*Peter chewed the end of his pencil **as he stared blankly** at the test in front of him.*

FURTHER EXAMPLES

As the bullets sprayed rapidly, Detective Mills ran for cover.
(Detective fiction)

As the hare slept soundly, the tortoise ambled past.
(Fable)

As the Earth formed slowly, the gods began to plant the seeds of mighty trees.
(Creation myth)

29 (V)ED NEXT (V)ED SENTENCES

EXAMPLES

Jake jumped out of bed and sprinted down the hall.
(Narrative)

The fearsome Minotaur sniffed the air and bared its bloodstained teeth.
(Myth)

The bear prepared its den and hibernated for the winter.
(Scientific recount)

EXPLANATION

Linked closely with the **eds and ings** sentence type, this stands apart due to the fact that the verbs are both *sequential* and *dependant*. The first part of the sentence describes an initial action using a past tense verb (one with an '**ed**' ending, hence the **(V)ed** name) :

*The bear **prepared** its den*

The second part of the sentence describes a subsequent action which occurs as a direct result of the first action. Another past tense verb - (V)ed - follows the connective 'and':

*The bear prepared its den and **hibernated** for the winter.*

TEACHING TIPS AND GENRE LINKS

This versatile sentence type extends the idea of dual action explored in the previous sentences by focusing on subsequent actions that demonstrate both cause and effect. It is easy to grasp and useful when considering appropriate verb and tense use (hence the **ed** of (**V**)**ed**).

One way to teach this sentence type is to let one action develop from another. Start with a question -

What did the character do?

Then following with either -

What did they do just before that? (an action that led to the action) or

What did they do straight after that? (A subsequent, related action)

For example:

What did the character do?

Jake sprinted down the hall.

What did he do just before that?

Jake jumped out of bed.

Combine the two:

Jake jumped out of bed and sprinted down the hall.

EXTENSION

Triple the action once again by adding a middle (**V)ed** (breaking the ed ending rule if necessary), and simply ensuring accurate use of past tense verbs throughout, as well as correct clause use, e.g.

*Rick turned on the spot, **dug his heels in** and raced after the robber.*

This could also provide the opportunity to discuss alliteration where the corresponding words are not directly juxtaposed, but linked by a feature. Challenge pupils to make the linking verbs begin with the same sound, e.g.

*I **climbed** up the ladder and **clambered** into the cockpit.*

*He **slipped** on the stairs and **slid** into the kitchen.*

*She **caught** the falling baby and **cradled** it in her arms.*

FURTHER EXAMPLES

I raced toward my presents and ripped off the paper.
(Diary)

I tiptoed down the hall and halted as it emerged before me.
(Ghost Story)

The mourners lifted the coffin and carried it slowly toward the church.
(Newspaper article)

30

THE QUESTION IS: SENTENCES

EXAMPLES

Jack disappeared. The question is: where did he go?
(Narrative)

Theron had betrayed his king. The question is: could he still be trusted?
(Legend)

Tutankhamen was the youngest Pharaoh ever. The question is: how did he die?
(Historical explanation)

EXPLANATION

This construction is actually composed of two sentences. The first is a short description of an action or statement of fact. The second begins with the phrase 'The question is:' followed by an intriguing question which draws the reader into the text.

TEACHING TIPS AND GENRE LINKS

Use the content of the first sentence to generate the question, or, take an intriguing hypothesis about the subject and introduce it by establishing the alternative in the first sentence:

The moon landing was the most important event of the 1960s. The question is: was it faked?

This sentence is also useful when considering both colons and the appropriate use of question marks.

EXTENSION

Consider adding a **list** of questions to intrigue the reader:

The moon landing was the most important event of the 1960s. The question is: was it faked? Did Neil Armstrong really walk on the moon? Or are the conspiracy theories correct?

FURTHER EXAMPLES

An area of forest equivalent to thirty-six football fields is cut down every minute. The question is: how can we stop this?
(Persuasive essay)

"The kingdom is a happy place. The question is: how long will it last?"
(Fairytale - dialogue)

The city streets were filled with desperate souls. The question is: who would save them?
(Graphic Novel)

THE MINOTAUR'S REVENGE
PHOTOCOPIABLE TEXT USING SENTENCE TYPES

The following text employs all of the sentence types in both this and the first book. As such it may be used as a deconstruction/discussion document which raises awareness of the many sentence types in the context of a whole text, whilst inspiring pupils by showing them what can be achieved using the approach.

We are currently writing a further book which includes examples of a broad range of genres (both fiction and non-fiction). In all instances the sentence types will be an integral aspect of the text.

To register interest in this book please email info@alanpeat.com using the subject 'New sentences and text types book'.

The Minotaur's Revenge

Imagine the most savage, vile beast you possibly can; a beast that most believed had been vanquished, a beast which somehow survived and is now thirsty for blood. This is the story of that very creature; the loathsome, demonic Minotaur.

Princess Ariadne was distraught, distraught because the man she loved had abandoned her. Theseus, who had sworn to marry Ariadne, had survived the Minotaur's labyrinth only because of her help and guidance. He had promised they would live together. Promised they would have a family, grow old, and die together. Yet no sooner had he escaped than he abandoned her on a desolate beach and sailed home to Athens. Sadness soon turned to rage: a fire burned within Ariadne that only the blood of Theseus could quench. The question was: how would she destroy this ungrateful fraudster? She knew the battle between Theseus and the Minotaur had been a close one...given a second chance, would the mighty beast prevail? Ariadne also knew that death was not final. Dying, in her world of gods and demigods, sorcerers and witches, was just another thing that, given the right knowledge and powers, could be undone. Ariadne was heartened - she knew exactly the right person to bring the Minotaur back to life. She schemed frantically and fervently. The more she plotted, the more darkly delighted she became...

Travelling across land and sea for three days, Ariadne finally approached the remote island where the palace of the sorceress Medea lay. Conditions were harsh, and she had suffered harshly, yet arriving at this magical place gave Ariadne a vast sense of relief. All her aches and pains disappeared as she tied her small boat to the pier; an old, rickety structure which looked as unstable as the waters which crashed around it. With a deep breath, she left the vessel and ventured tentatively forward along a narrow, wooded path. The princess was nervous: fingers trembling; legs shaking; tiptoeing along. The mysterious, magical, misty island murmured all around her, a fog seemed to have her in its grasp, tightening the higher she went, urging her to go back. Everything was strange, and Ariadne did not know what lay ahead. What she did know was that this was her only chance to get the revenge she so craved. Anxious yet determined, apprehensive yet resolute, she pushed on to the crest of the hill, and at the end of the path she finally saw the dark, foreboding palace. Ariadne forced herself to approach the door, stretched out her hand and knocked firmly three times. Wham! The door flew open all by itself! The princess jumped back as if she had seen a spectre. For a moment she considered running all the way back to her boat, until she felt the vengeful fire rise in her heart once more. Angered, emboldened, encouraged, she ventured through the open door into an opulent hall, where she came face to face with Medea, the sorceress. Medea was beautiful in a hypnotic, beguiling way; she dressed all in black, and her eyes seemed to pierce through to Ariadne's very soul as she spoke,

"What brings a pretty princess like you to a dangerous place like this?"

As she replied, Ariadne did her best to appear unafraid (inside, however, she was shaking like the rickety old pier that held her boat). As Medea glared at her, Ariadne told her about Theseus' betrayal. Listening in silence, Medea shuddered at the very mention of his name.

"That. Little. Brat! I tried to poison him years ago when he threatened to destroy my wonderful, happy home. If I didn't manage it, what hope does a princess with no powers have?"

"None, alone. But with your help I might resurrect the Minotaur, and use the beast to exact revenge, for myself, and for you."

"The Minotaur?" replied Medea as she approached Ariadne, a look of intrigue spreading slowly across her face. "They say the Marathonian bull was formidable, the Khalkotauroi even more dangerous, but the Minotaur was the most vile creature ever to walk the Earth. Perhaps, given another chance, it could serve our purpose. Take this, pour it on the beast's wounds, and be sure to stand well back..."

Carefully, Medea handed Ariende a vial of liquid which seemed to swirl with all the shifting shades of shadows at night. Bowing with respect, Ariadne turned and made her way quickly back to her boat, clutching the vial closely as the fog hurried her on.

Neither rough seas nor violent storms deterred Ariadne on her journey home to Crete. Under the cover of darkness she moored her boat and continued on to the entrance of the Minotaur's lair. Reaching into her satchel for the same ball of string she had given to Theseus, she tied the end to the doorpost and entered the labyrinth tentatively in search of the creature's body. The walls of the dimly lit maze oozed and swelled as if they too were hungry for flesh and could sense their next victim. It was easy to forget that not everyone who entered the lair died at the hands of the razor-toothed Minotaur. Some certainly met their end at the hands of the beast; others simply lost their way in the maze and died of starvation - in short it was a truly hellish place. Thankfully Daedalus, who was the architect of the labyrinth, had given Ariadne instructions which allowed her to find her way quickly to the centre. Entering the main chamber, she was overcome by the pungent smell of rotting flesh and spilled blood. The

Minotaur lay - lifeless and defeated - in the middle of the room.

"What an awful sight!" Ariadne thought. Steadying herself, she rose up slowly. "Strong, you must be strong. Remember why you are here," she repeated.

Slowly and carefully, steadily and purposefully, she approached the body and saw the gaping wound left by Theseus' sword. She stared at it as if this would be enough to reanimate the monster...even now she was unsure. What if it didn't work? What if the monster turned on her? What if she was left to rot here like so many in the past? Yet she thought of Theseus sailing away without her, and her burning, vengeful, strength returned. She poured the contents of the vial on the wound, stepped back, and waited.

For a time nothing happened, until Ariadne noticed the rough, split skin of the Minotaur seemingly knitting itself back together as if an invisible seamstress was at work. Dried blood became liquid again and drew back into the body. The more time that elapsed, the more life seemed to spread throughout the beast's body, yet still it did not move. Panicking, Ariadne began to pace back and forth - the potion had not worked! However, she was stopped dead in her tracks by a mighty bellowing roar which filled the chamber and caused her to clap her hands over her ears. The Minotaur exploded to its feet, beating its heavy chest, snarling and howling, then laid its fire-red eyes on the timid, shaking princess. As quickly as it had awoken, the creature charged at Ariadne, grabbed her by the throat and pinned her against the wall. It seemed as if she had made a terrible, terrible mistake...

However, the beast did not kill Ariadne. He simply stared straight at her, his demonic eyes meeting her terrified blue ones, and he knew in an instant what she had done for him. Setting her down gently, the Minotaur stepped away, bowing his head in a gesture of gratitude and submission. Ariadne was amazed - she approached the beast cautiously. She could feel the heat of his breath, the rage emanating from him, yet he kept perfectly still. As he bowed his head lower, Ariadne reached up and began to whisper in his ear her plan to destroy Theseus. With every word the Minotaur breathed more heavily; a growl that started in the pit of his stomach erupted uncontrollably at the end of Ariadne's speech. A malevolent smile spread across her face as she realised the Minotaur was with her, and would stop at nothing until Theseus was dead.

Leaving the Minotaur to rest and to gather its strength, Ariadne followed the string out of the labyrinth and hurried to her father, King Minos, to inform him of Theseus' survival. As the palace subjects gathered eagerly to listen, she stood before the King, whimpering pitifully while she told her version of the story. Ariadne was smart - she 'forgot' the part about helping Theseus in return for his hand in marriage, and instead convinced Minos that Theseus had kidnapped her, and had abandoned her on a beach once he felt his escape was assured. Minos was furious to hear that Theseus still lived, and that the Athenian blood-debt had not been paid; he'd never been so... humiliated. He was livid; his skin burned bright red; his fists shook violently as he spoke, and his voice tore through the crowds that had gathered...

"Hear my decree! Quickly, gather my ten finest warriors, they will set sail to Athens, and they will only return when Theseus is dead. I. Want. His. HEAD!"

And so, the squad of assassins was assembled within the hour. The leader, who was called Leophalies, had cold grey eyes, scars all over his body, and huge, powerful muscles which made him look as fierce as a charging rhinoceros. The other soldiers - swordsmen, archers and wrestlers - were just as savage: each one was a skilled, battle-hardened warrior responsible for the deaths of countless men. Brutish and vicious, yet skilled and organised, the squad knew their orders - they were to set sail the next morning. This suited Ariadne's plan perfectly...She waited until nightfall, then escaped the palace, returning once more to the labyrinth to collect the Minotaur.

In no time Ariadne was rushing out of the maze again, this time with the Minotaur following close behind. Under cover of darkness they left the city, dashing along the glistening, moonlit, silent beach to the dock which held the warriors' ship, 'The Paralus' aka the Bane of Athens for the many sons it had stolen from that city. They found a place on board The Paralus to conceal themselves, below deck, in the deepest area of the cargo hold. Enveloped by the hushed darkness, Ariadne went over the plan one more time...

"We travel at dawn, so the sunlight will signal our departure. With great care, we will maintain our secret presence and watch from a distance as our tormentor exhausts himself battling the fierce Cretan warriors. When Theseus - bloodied and broken - is at his weakest, we will reveal ourselves and attack. Inevitably the shock of seeing me, his forgotten love, and you, the now immortal Minotaur, as well as his exhausted state, will leave him defenceless; an easy target, and justice will be done!"

As before, the longer Ariadne spoke, the more agitated the Minotaur became, suppressing a great roar so much that he snapped the handle of the axe he was holding. Ariadne touched his shoulder lightly in an effort to calm him, and once she knew it was safe to do so, they both lay down, waiting for daybreak.

As the sun rose, the ship came alive with noise and movement: men loaded equipment onboard; crowds cheered the departing warriors; sails were raised and gentle waves carried the vessel out to sea. Battle cries and bellowed orders, the clashing of practice weapons and the crashing of the waves, all the cacophony hid the silent threat that lurked below deck. Concealed there was Princess Ariadne, her royal, broken heart now filled with deadly purpose and vengeance, and the slain beast, woken from the dead, thirsty for the blood of the man who had sent it to the gates of the underworld. There they remained, silent in the darkness, knowing that when the ship reached the shore, when the warriors were spent, when they finally revealed themselves to Theseus, then revenge would be theirs...

GUEST SENTENCES

Since the publication of the first book of sentence types we have been delighted to see that both teachers and pupils have invented many of their own. We have included a range of these here. Space restrictions mean that only a selection are presented, however we do thank everyone who took the time to write and experiment with sentences!

TEACHERS' SENTENCES

1. Verb Simile:

Towering like a wooden army, the giant Redwoods stood silently in the forest.

(Rob Smith)

2. Power of 3
   (Using 3 of any word class for emphasis)

He was strong, athletic and energetic - the perfect superhero!

(Rob Smith)

3. Two-place sentences

Underneath the newspaper, right beside the coffee cup, Annie saw what she had been looking for.

(Andrew Robinson, Shiphay Learning Academy)

4. Description, repetition

Oliver lifted his hands, his quivering bone-like hands.

(Kevin O'Brien, Thatto Heath Primary School)

5. HEADINGLEY sentences
   (Using -ed, -ing or -ly words to start a sentence.)

Excited, he set off on his journey.

Screaming, he fled from the Haunted House.

Cautiously, the batsman walked onto the cricket field.

(Phil Smith, Our Lady of Lourdes RC Primary, Leigh-on-Sea)

6. Something; something; something

Something was there; something was lurking; something was looking.

Something amazing was on the horizon; something I had never seen before.

(Shaun Hopper)

7. Something; someone

Something passed by me; someone was there.

(Shaun Hopper)

8. Whenever. Wherever. Whatever. (...in any order)

Whatever he did, things wouldn't be the same. Wherever he went, he would always be remembered. Whenever he looked back, the sadness would return.

(Kevin O' Brien)

9. Parallel phrase

Minute by minute the freezing, arctic breeze rises. Minute by minute death creeps closer to the lost explorers.

(Jim Armstrong. Shipston-on-Stour Primary School)

PUPILS' SENTENCES

1. 3 questions - statement

Who was at the door? Why were they here? What did they want from me?

I was soon to find out.

(Matt. Zoe Byrne's class, Mount Primary School, New Brighton)

2. 3ed De:de
(combining two sentence types from the first book of sentence types)

Exhausted, frustrated, bewildered, he chased after the box: he had to know what was inside

(Ted. Zoe Byrne's class Mount Primary School, New Brighton)

3. Using Some;others sentences to express different perspectives in a narrative

Mum thought we were all going to die; Dad thought we would survive; I didn't know what to think.

(Will: Zoe Byrne's class Mount Primary School, New Brighton)

4. Adverb, simile, action

Quickly, like a lightning bolt, he flew down the road, hoping he wouldn't miss school.

(Dean and Martin, Class 9, St. Richard's R.C. Primary School, Longsight)

Notes

WRITING EXCITING SENTENCES :
THE WHOLE SCHOOL APPROACH
(Reception - Year 6)
INSET TRAINING NOW AVAILABLE
with ALAN PEAT

CLUSTER TRAINING COSTS

Two schools clustering: **£800** per school, **three** schools: **£700** per school.
Four schools: **£650** per school.

Plus **£95** towards local accommodation where applicable for the night prior to the event, plus 'at cost' travelling expenses. Handouts are charged at 60p per person.
For larger numbers fees are negotiated directly with Alan.

IF SCHOOLS WISH TO SELL OUT ADDITIONAL PLACES TO STAFF FROM SURROUNDING SCHOOLS TO OFFSET COSTS, WE ASK THAT THEY CHARGE NO MORE THAN **£100** PER PLACE.

We add an additional **£60** for each place 'sold on' and the school retains **£40**.

This brand new conference will begin by exploring how to develop 'sentence sense' in Early Years contexts and Key Stage 1 before concentrating on Alan's 'consistent language' approach (Level 2-Level 5).

The day draws on ideas in 'Writing Exciting Sentences' (Alan Peat 2008) and 'A Second Book of Exciting Sentences' (Alan Peat and Mathew Sullivan 2013) as well as Alan's research based on school audits he has undertaken nationally.

Packed with practical ideas to take and use immediately, Alan will also consider how best to implement and manage a sustainable whole-school approach to developing a grammatically correct breadth of sentence types.

Amazed, astounded, astonished, I had never seen so many children willingly use these effective, powerful sentences.
@ICTMrP

The sentence types are a perfect springboard. Once the children understand them, the only limit is their imagination. Putting grammar and punctuation in context, then giving it a memorable name: so simple but so effective.
@ZoeByrne

To book: call 07789938923 or email: info@alanpeat.com